Thank You Life!

A Self-Help

SANSKRITI BHATT

notionpress
.com

INDIA · SINGAPORE · MALAYSIA

ISBN
Paperback: 979-8-89186-532-7
Hardcase: 979-8-89233-349-8

I Am Writing this Book

Because I Want to Cherish the Understanding
My Life Situations Have Given Me.

"*Thank-You Life*" For Being So Beautiful.

By

Sanskriti Bhatt

Contents

Contents

Contents

Contents

Acknowledgement

I acknowledge everyone who has been a part of my journey of life from the very first day.

My parents, teachers, friends, grandparents, relatives, well-wishers, and everyone who has been a continuous source of support, my team of Padma Siddhi Films, and the unconditional love of my dear sheriff.

Introduction

TO ALL MY READERS,

This book is no masterpiece, and the words in it are none other than the ones you hear daily. I am 23 years old and an actress. My debut film, SAUMYA GANESH, didn't release until I started writing this book. Apart from that, I stepped into the world of cinema from the Hindi film Sumeru, swiftly added to my bag without a second thought. Sumeru did not turn out to be a success in the showbiz world. I was accused of not being "heroine-material". Sorry to mention, but at that point, I realised that we humans consider ourselves as "material" and not "human". My team and I had been under the constant pressure of failure and many such accusations, and my family was under the pressure of "what would happen next?"

At this moment, I gave myself a second thought and believed what I did was surely no blunder, but it wasn't a success either. So, what was it? The answer was quite lengthy, so I wrote it right here. This book contains my love and thoughts that have taught me to live a simpler life and help myself to be empowered every day, even on the broken days life brings to me, hence making it beautiful. I "THANK YOU, LIFE". Sometimes, life will not make you struggle to teach the persistence it requires. It might give you hiccups and tell you to buck up. It's better you understand it wisely because it is "us" who make the right choice at the right time, choosing everything that is meant for "us", even our failures and success. In today's world, we find people unsatisfied, unhappy, grumpy, bossy, and full of complexities, be they inferior or superior. My failures helped me resolve these thoughts. I've received many messages of appreciation and love for my performance in my film, and I'm really grateful for that, my audience.

The chapters in this book are the lessons I learned over this period, starting from my teens until today. Someone wise and close to my heart told me that I was the reflection of their penned imagination, and I felt that. In this book, the therapies I use daily are what I'm sharing with you. Hope you find the best answers to thank everything you have and not hold on to the things that are missing in your life. May you find everything that you have been looking for.

Set Out for Your Dreams!

"Life will always push you in the direction of your dreams."

I often wonder whether the world is too small for my dreams or if my dreams are way too huge for the world. Let me tell you,

Being hopeful has never left me hopeless,

Being selfless has never left me heartless,

Being happy with what I have has never turned out to be a part of mourning,

Being neglected has never left me contemplating and doubting myself, and

Being honest has never left me guilty.

Today, I encourage you to be hopeful, selfless, happy, self-confident, and honest.

Look at the positive outlook on everything, and trust me, they never end up disappointing you.

Follow your dreams live up to your expectations, and remember that it is okay to be hard on yourself whenever required because you are the only one who knows how capable you are.

Believe in yourself and trust your judgements; just set out for your dreams!

THEY ARE YOURS, WHEN EVERYONE ELSE GIVES UP.

Realise

This might sound weird, but it is the truth. When was the last time you realised a mistake? Five hours before you started reading this book? Or maybe at this moment. Realisation comes when you accept the mistakes you made and not by pinpointing the mistakes others make. Once you "real-eyes" your own weaknesses, everything starts evolving around you. The best version of realising is "self-realisation", and once you start with this, you surely are on the path to getting the answers you've been looking for. It might take a moment because realisation is no impulsive reaction; it takes time and understanding.

We often neglect the things that help us meet our inner selves, but we do prioritise the things that are quite far away, hence missing the good things around us and not realising it in time.

Let me give you an example: on a cold winter day when everything seems to be freezing, you keep on pinpointing the weather for being so rude, but in the end, after a day full of criticising nature, you "realise" that you have been constantly criticising something that couldn't be changed and hence not seeing with "real-eyes" in real-time. You fill yourself with negative thoughts all day and make yourself frustrated.

Now, how do you change this habit of yours? Very simple but requires willingness. Willingness to accept and change, your mental illness of constantly looking for what you don't have. Yes, it is an "illness" that rushes pressure in the tiny blood cells of your body, and we obviously neglect these tiny little things, but forget that these little cells are the "basic unit of life". So, the choice is yours, and even the willingness is yours; you want to change and see everything with "real-eyes" in time, or you want time to make you realise everything. Mind me, it's never too late to realise.

Thankful

Being thankful for everything is another key to resolving your problems, and for that, you need to have a "tank full" of patience and humbleness. Keep your hopes grounded; it helps you to grow with the hope that you have, from your loved ones, your colleagues, or anyone you are dealing with.

You might be thinking that you are often thanking people, but you don't realise when you become thankless. Ever had this thought? Maybe yes or maybe not. You don't need to worry; it is the most common problem we face today, where people think that they are being thankful, but unknowingly they become thankless. It is because of the rush we are in, and we barely give ourselves time to think and process.

So, there is something I need to tell you about this. We often try to tell our surroundings that we possess them, and we forget to thank them for being there. We shower all our love and happiness upon them, but we neglect their requirements and their love, and when we do not get the same output from their side as we expect, we start being thankless because our drop of patience is on the tip of our vessel, and it causes a rush of emotions, and humbleness, being the most "humble", is left somewhere at the end due to that rush.

Have you ever thought of being impulsive yet calm? This may seem like something out of the blue, but it is not. You have to have your emotions, but you have to know how your tongue reacts to it. The "tongue" is the only sense organ out of the five sense organs (eyes, nose, ears, skin, and tongue) that is trapped in our mouth, which means it is a prisoner of our mind and won't come out till the mind tells it to. You can have an impulsive mind, but your tongue can be calm.

You start vomiting out everything that comes to your mind; it empties your "tank", and your "tank-full" becomes a "tank-less". Now the question is, how do you overcome it? You can, and you will, once things stop bothering you, and firstly, you stop bothering yourself. You can simply be more focused on what makes you feel bowed, thankful, and happy, rather than looking for someone else to be happy and thankful for what you do. Trust me, no one does that unless you do it yourself. So, process what is in your mind; it takes time for the impulse to reach your tongue, and on the way, it can be changed, the way you change your clothes unless you get satisfied with the outfit you're wearing to go out is perfect! The same goes for the words you use to express your mind; be patient and humble.

Believe and Belief

A small belief can make big things happen, but for that, you have to believe in the moment and focus on your belief. A belief can turn into reality only when you chant it with liveliness. Having a belief does not mean you start turning it down once it does not turn up at the right time. You might have noticed that if you do not stand up to the expectations of your own people, their belief starts turning up as anxieties, worries, mood swings, and many more feelings that shake you from top to bottom. This is the moment when you have to be charged and believe in your thoughts. You gotta reconfirm yourself about every damn belief of yours because you choose it, and no one else is going to live your belief. It is you in the end who will live with that belief and achieve because of that belief you once believed in. A belief often looks like a "lie" in its spelling, but it is just like the unspoken and unachieved truth. So have a belief until the time it becomes a belief, and you start living with it.

Success

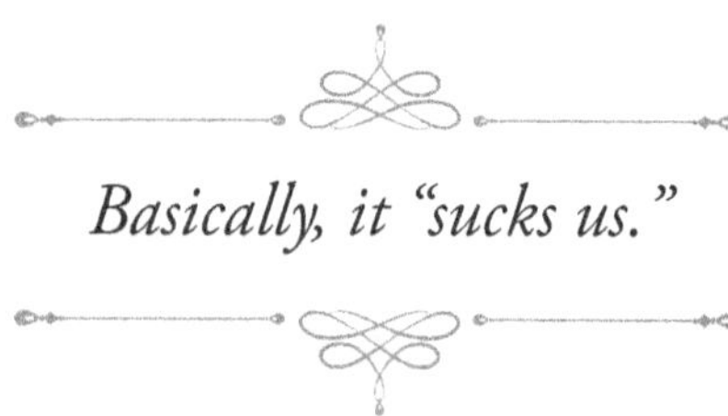

Basically, it "sucks us."

What is success for us? A simple yet difficult question to answer. Have you ever thought why is it so? Have you ever thought about what success for you is?

Too many questions to ask and one answer to give: your point of satisfaction is your peak of success. The saddest tendency of a man is to be unsatisfied at every point.

You can barely measure success; every goal we've set and accomplished is a success in its own way. The thought of being successful "sucks us", completely because anything you do requires hard work, focus, and effort which you yourself have to do. Some people start good and end up with nothing.

The journey to success is that of a young kid walking to school on a hot summer day. The sun seems to suck your energy; it is the same thing. As a kid, you are focused, you walk your way, and you know that it is the time, but as we grow older, we set ourselves free. We run away from the things that suck our energy on our way to our goal, and we get back to our comfort zones.

As a kid, we never did this; we always finished our goals no matter what and how difficult they seemed to be.

You don't remember, but you even managed your first steps; you stood by yourself. Everything you compare in life is somewhat interlinked, but we make things complicated, success is nothing but a repeated loop, and you have to maintain consistency like you did on the first step of yours.

Success is basically being satisfied, and let me tell you, being satisfied does not mean it's the last attempt you've made for something.

Once you are satisfied with something, that means you've completed one step of success, and you keep on adding steps to your ladder of success. It cannot be defined at one particular point or at one achievement.

Success continues for a lifetime; it has no end. It continues until the time you want it to be a part of your journey of life.

24

Making Others Happy?

"Everything you achieve is a part of your happiness."

It's never been easy to ease people; it's never been easy to love what others love; it's never been easy to do anything.

But yes, there is something I want you to know: things are the way you treat them to be.

Either ease them or let the uneasy disturb you.

After being left unrecognised after my film, I "realised". Every step you take might not be a success for your well-wishers; every promise you make might not be kept, and it's okay.

You tried with honesty, and that's enough because every plan isn't a success. There are times when your expectations will not prove to be what others expect from you.

Anything you accomplish is for your betterment. Yes, you surely can listen to the advice given to you, but decide what makes you happy, and choose what comforts you.

Now see, whatever you do, there will be people around you who will seek the unaccomplished and not the accomplished.

So just keep up with the best you can do; don't just give up because their thoughts pull you back.

The very first thing you have to do is define yourself to yourself because you intuitively know when and where you go wrong.

If you try to make others happy, you might lose your emotional balance, which results in massive breakdowns.

I've had one, and it was painful because I tried to accept the opinion people had about my film, but I ignored how we tried to acquire every single frame of it.

I just stopped thinking about the happiness it gave me to see myself on various platforms, and this is where I went wrong.

I chose others' opinions over my hard work, and that is where I left myself unrecognised.

I don't want you to do it; everything you achieve is a part of your happiness.

Humanity

We humans, started a race, and the behaviour of that race was called "humanity."

After my 12th, I was destined to be a part of a journey I was unknown to, and it had been really difficult, dealing with people having different stereotypes, different opinions, different judgements, and whatnot.

We humans have about 99.9%, and it is only the 0.1% that creates this difference—good or bad, happy or sad, anger or calmness, and every damn difference.

Humans create miracles because they themselves are one, "a creation of the unseen miraculous power", isn't it?

But we create a difference, taking our own lives through biological wars, chemical wars, weapons, harsh behaviour, and much more; the list is endless.

You must have felt the changes in the behaviour of the people around you if you do not get down to the expectations they had for you.

We often fail to agree with the 99.9% we have the same, but we always look at the 0.1% difference we have.

Be the master, Be brave

"The highest in the hierarchy."

Have you ever considered your decisions to be wrong before executing them? Have you ever given yourself a chance to correct it? We often try to correct people, but somewhere deep inside, we never try to replace or modify our thoughts.

We are scared of changing that one mindset that we have, and we stick to it. We simply put ourselves in a tub full of adhesive and stick to that one thing we've made up in our minds.

Let me tell you, it doesn't show your bravery; it simply shows your ineligibility to deal with the different powers inside you. Your thoughts are your power, and if any thought troubles you, it means the power of that particular thought is seeking your energy, and it can be changed. Yes! Your thoughts can be changed; they can be modified, and you can find peace within yourself.

Does that sound difficult?

If yes, then you haven't understood what your thoughts are, or you assume your thoughts to be your master in every path you choose. If yes, you are brave enough, and you have chosen to be a master of your thoughts, and a master in any form is the highest in the hierarchy.

True Happiness

Whenever we fail to appreciate the simplest things in life, we ignore the happiness around us. We always look at the empty frames, but we never look into the frames that are full of moments and life. Honestly, even when I'm writing this, I feel unhappy, I feel sad, and I feel that things around me are not my type, but at the same time, I understand that it is never going to be what I want it to be.

My mind feels fucked, totally out of state, but then I realise the purpose of the sadness and believe me, it's never me.

In the same way, you just try and realise what is it that is taking you away from your satisfaction, your happiness; you'll understand how dumb you have been when you're looking for the worst state of satisfaction in your life.

True happiness? The question arises. It is within you. The answer arrives. You can never look up to someone or someone else's thoughts to be your happiness, but yes, you can be a part of their thoughts and their life if you are happy to do so. No one is stopping you in any way; it is your way of attracting the happiness you have been looking for.

In the same way, you need to attract the energies from the things that are around you but, you usually end up attracting the energies that are not around you, hence crying for things that are not with you, and you neglect the happiness you get from the things around you. Value what serves you. Trust me, it will make you feel healthier and happier, always, and that is what your "true happiness" is. You have it with you; you just have to recognise it at the right moment.

Wisdom

"Keep your powers divided."

The true hallmark of wisdom is nothing but the separation of your physical and psychological powers. As mentioned before, your power is your thought, and we humans have different powers, and the two main powers are physical and psychological.

Now, how do you separate the two powers from the same body?

See, your mind is a labour of your thoughts, and your thoughts are an outcome of the understanding you get from your surroundings. Notice your behaviour; your physical behaviour defines your psychological state.

I bet you never would have behaved differently when it comes to a sad psychological state; you won't care even if it's a public place. Now, this is where you gotta make a wise choice. You cannot always let your psychological impulse overtake your physical state.

Here is when you have to keep your powers divided; you can't just vomit out every stupid thought that comes to your mind. Give time to your impulses.

You Are Light

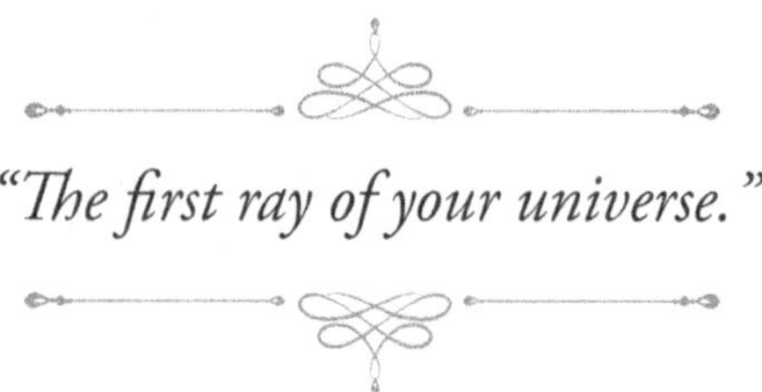

"The first ray of your universe."

"The light" of your world, the hope of your dreams is you. The intensity of your thoughts lights up the path towards your goals. The torchbearer of your plans is you; yes, you might have supporters and followers, but in the end, it is you who has to put his or her hand on the peak of your goal.

Anyone can push you, or hold you, but the torch is in your hand; you have to keep it upright, on the right path.

Whenever a day ends, you will realise that no one was as intensified as you were, as glorifying as you were. But every morning, you expect everyone else around you to be as radiant as you are, and you look up to them as the torchbearer, and you forget how "LIT" you have been.

Never forget yourself; never forget your light because you are the first ray of your universe.

Be Like Someone?

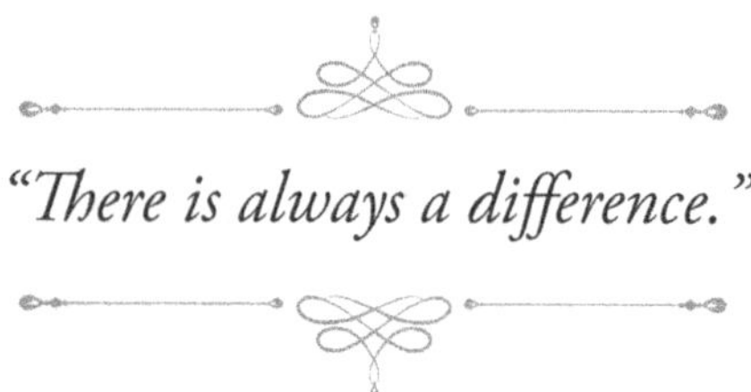

"There is always a difference."

Honestly, as a girl, I never wanted to be like my mother too, and if not "maa", I would never want to be "someone".

You know, my mother was meant to be mine, so she is the best for me; my teachers were meant to be the best for me, so I learned from them.

But if I become one of them, the energy clashes, and I am not like them, but I am better for the universe they formed for me and the surroundings they gave me.

Further, I would form a new universe where I will be a mother, a teacher, a mentor, and every relationship we share as humans.

We can't be the same don't worry about it. Any relationship you are sharing is pure and divine; if one falls, the other picks up; if the other breaks down, the other will make them stand. We have different qualities.

You and I have fluctuations in our thoughts and emotions. I don't use the word different because poles are apart and different, and two poles can never walk the same journey, and even if they do, there is always a difference.

Let Go

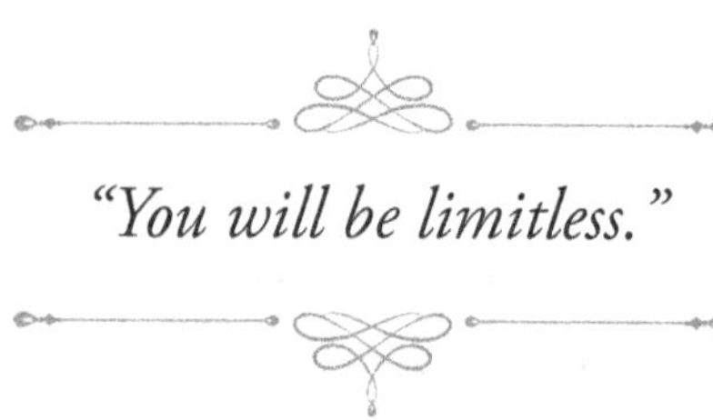

Letting go does not mean stopping caring or ignoring.

Letting go means "this too shall pass". It means you are willing to release the things that are harming you.

Don't "let go" of your thoughts, but "let go" of the surroundings that constrict you from reaching your thoughts.

Lord Krishna once said, "Those who stay restricted stay restrained, and those who shatter themselves, discover the limitless."

So let go of what restricts you and shatter yourself to your thoughts, believe them, and you will be limitless.

Always remember, the deeper you dive, the more you discover, and the better you touch the surface because you tend to reach the limitless, whether you dive in the sea or sky.

Simplicity

"Difficult does not make the cult."

We often try to get into complexities that restrict us, be they inferior or superior. We always get into a trap and make it difficult.

If you make it difficult, that does not mean it will be "cult." Even if it is simple, it can be good. Keep in mind that it has to be clear.

What makes it difficult is that it is not clear; there are lots of obstacles that are making it unclear. The obstacles are your fears and your complexes.

I am not saying to always choose the simpler path. What I'm trying to tell you is that you can stop manifesting what is making it difficult and keep up with what drives you to your goal.

Sometimes the simplest thoughts create magic, and the thoughts that make noise are left dumb and unspoken.

You must have noticed that the simpler you think, the better you execute, or the better you speak. Once you make them complex, you know what happens.

Basically, what you say simply is what you truly think, and what you don't is the complication of thoughts you create in your mind, which leaves you unspoken.

So keep it simple and be "cult".

Know Your Path

"It is okay to break down; you will, and you can stand up again and walk ahead."

You have been blessed with your mind and heart—the mind that leads you by logic and the heart that leads you by emotions.

Your path requires both, and you should know how to balance them. No one will enjoy your success the same way no one will put in the effort that you do.

While walking the way, you will realise that everyone is walking their paths individually; it doesn't matter if they stay with you; remember, they don't walk with you; they don't dream with you.

Everyone has their individual goals, their mind that leads them by logic, and their heart that restricts or shatters their emotions.

The mind has no other option than our heart, which makes a difference in every individual's thought. The four chambers of our heart produce four different ways of living.

Our mind, on the other hand, is responsible for the mechanism of our body, but the life in that body is because of our heart.

So, the choice is yours: if the brain fails to function, use your heart; if the heart stops, use your brain.

If both collapse, know that you're on the right path. If you ever break, because you can come out of it, your mind still has the courage, and your heart has the strength to deal with it. Now that you know the path, just walk your path with your zeal. It is okay to break down; you will, and you can stand up again and walk ahead.

Understanding the Best

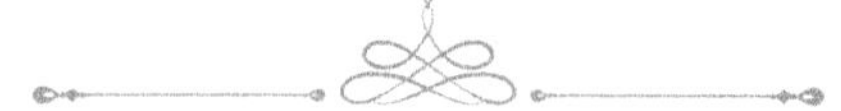

Always have the thought of being misunderstood?

Every moment you feel so, have you ever thought about what you missed in your conversation?

Whenever there is a conversation between two or more people, there is a chance of being misunderstood because the thoughts clash.

You should have the stability to get over the thoughts that harm your inner feelings; you can simply pick up the best.

It's not always the best but remember that every conversation is like a cube; the sides of a cube are directly proportional to a single thought. Think about it; you will get to know the different meanings and ways of one thought. It ultimately depends on you what you choose, the best or the worst.

The better you think for yourself, the better you will understand. The complexities develop when you start getting into the thoughts of others; you have your own thoughts, find what is best for you, and you will understand the best from others too.

It's a magic mantra that will work for sure.

Intolerance

Intolerance has now become a disease that is curable, but we give up whenever it comes to curing it.

One day or another, you might have felt things or situations that were intolerable; that is common these days. Every common man has nothing but intolerance. One bright sunny day at the traffic light, I was waiting for the red light, and there was a man who was constantly honking. I moved my scooter aside and swung my arm to show him the way. I don't know why, but that man stopped and shouted at me. For a minute, I felt like shouting back, but then I started laughing, sadly, at his face. He pointed at me and rushed his car ahead.

I laughed; that was the moment I realised I had nothing to do with the man, but he had something to do with me, probably to make me realise that I have the power of tolerance for the foolish things we do as humans.

I did nothing, but I started realising my self-worth. Now, realising your worth does not mean you have to see everyone as superior. It means you should know what you deserve and how capable you are. Only if you know your capability can you know what is meant for you. It's like a platter you're being served, and you have to pick what attracts you the most. One day or another, you pay for whatever you choose: that's the truth. Pick from intolerance to tolerance; it totally depends on you. But remember, intolerance only makes your buttocks heavy.

Winner Since Birth

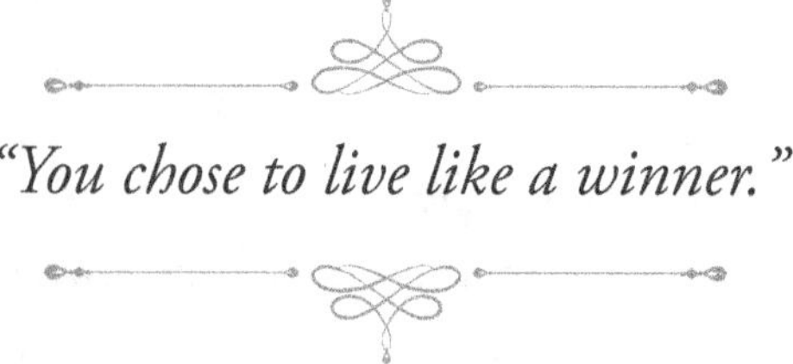

"You chose to live like a winner."

Doubting yourself? Scared of the "what ifs" in life

What if you don't achieve your goal?

What if you give up?

What if you don't earn as much as you expect?

What if! What if! And what the F!

You know you're a winner, even after all these questions and doubts.

You are much more developed than a sperm. You are the winner out of those millions that once entered your mother's womb.

You just had a head and a tail; now that you have your body, you fail to understand your worth.

Always know this,

1. You survived out of the millions.

2. You sustained it for nine months.

3. You survived the delicate days after birth.

4. You didn't die of malnutrition.

5. You are still breathing after all the ups and downs you went through.

6. You choose to LIVE like a WINNER.

So be grateful for what you have.

Karma

We define karma as "You did this to me; the same shall happen to you!"

Honey, this isn't karma. This is something like casting black magic. If something wrong happens to us, we blame the situation; if something bad happens to others, we accuse them of the Karma blame game. Oh, this happened to her or him because she or he did this and that wrong.

The reality is that Karma has its own definitions according to every human's beliefs and dimensions of understanding.

We are humans, and we make mistakes, knowingly or unknowingly, and whenever we make mistakes, we never keep in mind that anything bad will happen to us.

I personally believe that karma plays the least important role in the race for success.

Even if a terrorist attains the supremist success of his "goal," no matter if he kills a million and what he receives is a single death, sometimes a man who hasn't even touched an ant receives nothing his whole life and eventually dies an unknown death. So, can you say what you missed out on in life is because of the "karma" you did?

Karma only means do the needful of whatever you are willing to attain, and no one wishes to attain, and embrace a life full of frustrations and problems.

Live and Let Live

Life, one way or another, brings you to the situation of not giving any clarification over anything you are being accused of.

You know, we often try to control the people around us, but deep inside we know we can't do that. We cannot take over someone's mind unless they allow us to, and I have seen in so many relationships that one person tries to impose his or her thoughts on the other person. It feels good to keep a new relationship going, but it cannot keep a relationship going.

I truly understand that the urge to keep your loved ones close is to care about them, but that doesn't mean we stop them from exploring the world they created for themselves; that doesn't mean we try to control them over the things and experiments we feel are wrong.

Everyone has their own perspective, and with that, we prepare and work accordingly. When

I'm talking about relationships, it refers to every relationship we share in our lives.

If the best moments we have are the ones where we explore ourselves, then how can we have control over someone else's way of living? Can't we just live and let live?

The best thing I can let you know is to keep your patience and your anxieties to yourself. What happened to you is not meant for them. Everyone has their own journey and their own style of living, so just let live.

Where is Mankind?

Start giving in; mankind is dying, and so are you.

There is a question mark; do you know why? Because you ask this every time you're left in the middle of nowhere, once my dear friend told me, "You cannot make everyone happy, so leave everything as it is!" I've always disagreed with this idea of fake condolence.

Yes, "fake condolence", This is what you advise someone when you cannot help them come out of the hardships they're facing. Knowingly or unknowingly, you often give such advice, and most of you, without any doubt, work on this advice.

But have you ever thought that one action of making someone happy at their point of discouragement could overpower the sorrow of their soul? You could teach someone to be hopeful rather than hopeless; you could help someone to be stable during any breakdown in their life; instead, what you do is give them a temporary inhuman solution, that is, "Leave everything as it is!".

To be honest, you could have helped the other person to cheer up and help them fight the situation that life brings to them. But what we have learned is to just focus on ourselves and our own happiness, but we forget that sharing happiness and making someone happy during hardships can make this world a better place to live.

So stop ignoring and start opening yourself; start giving in; mankind is dying, and so are you.

Importance of Silence

"Silence is orally overrated and practically underrated."

Whenever I ask someone to be quiet in a room full of chaos, I receive "offensive" gratitude in return.

In a world where everyone is running after something and asking for something in return, no one chooses silence. Honestly, silence heals, and the only reason people are more distracted and less focused is that we have so much to "Chap-Chap" about.

Ever seen a lion? Or heard of it? He has stillness and calmness before he grabs his prey. This is the stillness of silence. Ever had diarrhoea? Or heard about this condition? It is the excess waste your body throws away, sometimes the useful ones too, and this causes weakness. In the same way, excessive diarrhoea of words can weaken your body and mind.

There is an exercise all of us need to practice. First of all, just stop shouting in the morning when you wake up and never wake the other person like there's an earthquake. Practice silence for at least half an hour in the morning, and even if you want to speak out, do it calmly and not with impulsiveness. It hurts your soul.

The power of silence is orally overrated and practically underrated. The only reason it is underrated is because you start teaching others to be silent, you start practicing yourself, and you see how fast everything around you evolves.

Calm Yet Impulsive

Whatever you wish to attain in your life, some people like it the basic way, while others search for the extraordinary; both are choices that have different outcomes.

But I suggest you make either of the choices with impulsive calmness or calm impulsiveness.

You know both words complement each other; the only thing that differs is the psychology of understanding—to understand a better version of every vision.

You should know the point of calmness of your mental state; not every situation has to be given full attention by your personal impulses. Your mellow state of mind leads to the proper usage of the nerves that create impulses in your brain.

Hence, impulsiveness is something that keeps you calm and intact with your body.

Deal with problems while keeping your spirits high and calm at the same time, because every time you try and burst out with any kind of impulse, you make things complex.

Try this once. Even when you feel like you need to burst out, keep it inside, let it settle with a deep breath, and make yourself feel like you're better than ever. You get things more wisely now, and trust me, you'll be calmer than ever with the never-ending high impulses that keep your spirits on top always!

Straightforward or insensitive?

*"If you have the courage to speak,
have the courage for a straight listening too."*

The difference between these two words is huge, but the meaning is what determines our understanding.

Sometimes we assume ourselves to be straightforward but forget about how insensitive we become at the same moment.

There's a way of expressing and conveying your words in mannerism; there's always a point when we neglect how unruly we become. I know your oesophagus gives you reflexes to bring the shit out of your pit, but not everyone is ready to take it.

Being straightforward is appreciated and will always be, and there are two ways of recognising yourself as one:

(a) You just blast your inner tornado and try to keep your hand up, don't bother to listen to what the other person says, and forcibly try to proceed with your decisions.

(b) You keep your views forward and listen to what the agreements and disagreements are; you speak out for something that is still out of your dimension.

If you have the courage to speak, have the courage for straight listening too.

Pointing out with one finger isn't straightforward; remember that the other three point towards you. Forget about others, but you're being insensitive to yourself too.

Think about it; maybe you can still correct yourself; if not, cut this page and move on.

Find a Way Forward

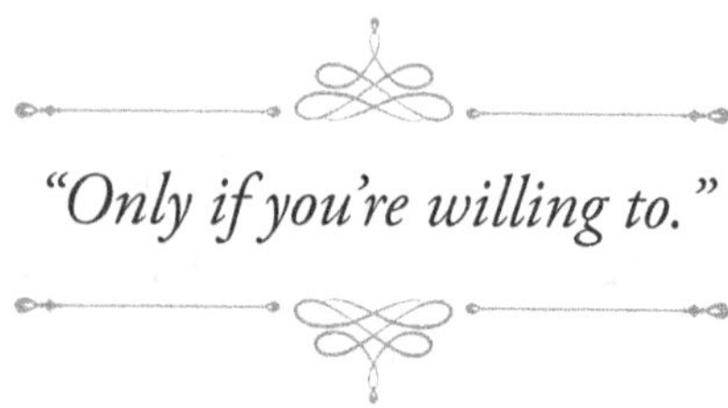

There are things that hold us back. Someday or another, we try to move forward, but some of our strings hold us back. We have so many reasons to hold ourselves back and just one reason to keep ourselves going. Of course, we have a lot of priorities once we reach a certain point of achievement, but before that, we have a "step-by-step" way of attaining what we want. Nothing comes to us without struggle or without preparing to struggle for it.

You know, whenever you look back, you will find so many things you missed and plenty of opportunities you let go, and I bet you will blame the circumstances or situations for them.

88% of people I met have the same issues or are dealing with the same anxiety: "They could've done this, but this or that thing stopped them".

The remaining 2% don't understand what they have missed or what they have done to themselves, and the last 10% are the ones who know the management of human functionalities.

To the 88%, I would suggest that what is gone will never come back, but what is left is yours, and you're spoiling it by dragging and chanting the things you missed. STOP IT, GUYS! You still have so much to do, and so much you can still do.

The 2% won't get what I'm saying, so dude, you be the sloth of your life and be it what it is; it is good for everyone around you, hence keeping things good for you too. If you want to, you can get out of it, but ONLY IF YOU ARE WILLING TO. You can be the 10% too.

10% ones, you have been managing it quite well, but if you lose the consistency and your practice of doing your "karma" daily, you will soon be included in the 88%. So just keep yourself calm and keep going because things will break you, but you have to keep striving to improve the percentage around you, and if everything around you improves, you too get better, you stop regretting, you start finding your own ways, and you start building yourself better and better on your terms and conditions. Inclusive is all the family and self-happiness you have been looking for, but honestly, let me tell you, IT TAKES TIME AND CONSISTENCY.

Power of Imagination

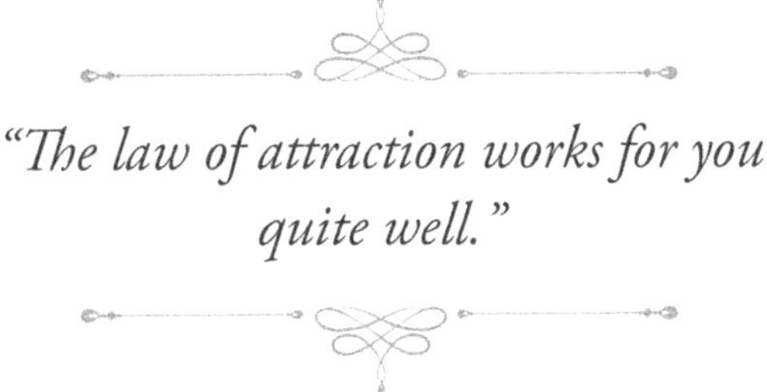

The mentality of a toddler is said to be the most imaginative. Well, that's true. As we grow, we are so preoccupied with pressures that we end up thinking the same way as the community around us thinks. I'm not talking about society; it is much greater than a community. You are basically bound by the community of people you are surrounded by.

As children, we never think of such things, but as we grow older, it is instilled in our minds that there is a limitation to what we imagine or what we desire in our lifetime.

What you become when you grow up is the construction of your thoughts, so be aware of what you imagine yourself to be.

I, as a child, had always imagined myself performing in front of people, but I was an introvert, so I stopped myself. But my imagination is taking me closer to my goal of being what I always wanted to be in my subconscious space.

The journey seemed easy to me and easier to the people around me, but trust me, my imagination took everything out of me, every bit of energy and hard work.

So, even if you imagine, you have to pull up your socks and just keep the target right at the centre, and the law of attraction works for you quite well.

Remember that the energies you attract will work for you, no matter how.

Don't Stop

Sometimes, when we look back, we see our footprints—how far we have come—and they remind us of the pathways we choose for ourselves and how hard or easy it has been to walk through all of them.

Moments and circumstances will always pull you back, but what matters is that you have walked a step every moment, and that is enough.

I know things will never fall into place, and that is what will irritate you the most. What I have always done is keep it inside me, keeping my weaknesses and fighting on my own. I know you will feel like bursting in front of every person you know in this world, but not every time you'll have someone to speak to, not every time someone will make way for your thoughts to enter their mind and body.

Ultimately, you will find a way for yourself and cope with whatever you're going through. Because you analyse yourself better than anyone, you are going to judge your journey, and you are the ultimate winner of the race you've been running alone. Remember, if you stop, you will find it hard to start again, but if you walk step by step, when you look back, there will be a part that you've covered, and you've moved slightly closer to your GOALS.

Positivity

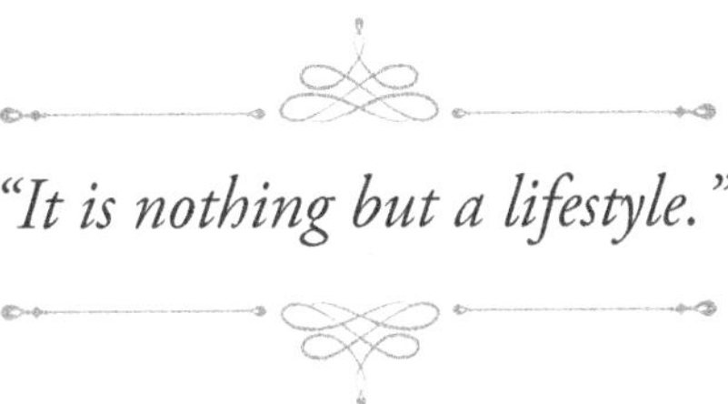

"It is nothing but a lifestyle."

We are always taught to be positive, which is absolutely appreciated at many points in our lives.

I have seen people who pretend to be positive. But there is always a difference between staying positive and forcing positivity. I don't know how to put this into good words, but yes, you need to feel positive from within before you teach what it is. You simply make positivity your lifestyle, and things will change around you. Stop seeing the bad or negative consequences before even putting in the effort to make it good. It is very basic in human nature, especially in parental nature, that they see the good, but the bad and negative content has a greater impact on their brain, which is really energy draining.

All I would suggest is to keep doing things with good effort and don't do it for a good result because you might fail too. JUST DO IT because you want to, and because you are willing to give your best, things will fall into place.

Keep manifesting and practicing your deeds; when it becomes a part of your lifestyle, positivity will find its place in your life.

Prioritise the Self

There will be situations and people dominating you; there will be words that will hurt you, but you know what? The things that pull you back are the ones that give you the aggression to move forward.

We are often told to deal with the situation and with others, but we aren't taught how to deal with ourselves. We teach others, but we forget to nurture ourselves. This is the point of being "uneducated" towards ourselves because we never studied our body and soul. The change that we expect from the people around us first has to be accepted by ourselves. We need to prioritise ourselves so that we can heal ourselves.

Prioritising ourselves does not mean becoming narcissists; it means being good enough to correct yourself and improve at every step. Instead of ordering and bossing over others, you need to prioritise your feelings of understanding and managing things that bother you.

You can do this only if your brain is open to all directions of learning; otherwise, you can just sit with the rigid mindset you've got, which is already driving you crazy!

So cheers to learning and exploring "self".

Analyse Yourself

There are so many things happening around us every day; in some way or another, we doubt ourselves, we overthink, and that is how things start affecting us.

There will be moments that will break you and pull you from both ends, but that is the real point of analysing yourself.

At moments, we start blaming others or taking things to heart, but we forget to rectify ourselves, and rectifying does not mean doubting. Rectifying is knowing where you have been wrong towards yourself and getting better once you know it.

The things that affect us are because we overthink about them, and then we start responding to the overthought "thoughts" that we have created in our minds, and in extreme cases, people do harm themselves.

We need to have a strong point at the peak of every problem because that is the point when you start breaking and then you shatter.

So analyse your self-worth and stop responding to things that affect you negatively, because they're just temporary phases that will end sooner or later and aren't as important as your own self.

Deal With People

"Just open your arms wide for the time they're looking for someone."

See, we live in a world where we cannot avoid everything. There are some things and some situations that we have to face and deal with pragmatically.

Now how to deal is the question. See, not every time you can correct people just because the situation is wrong according to you, and this is where you start hampering yourself. Maybe this is the sign of being the dominant one too, but most of the time it is when you're too scared about the people around you, and we need to understand that everyone around us is a grown-up and self-dependent person, so we need not poke and protect them for certain reasons of anxiety we have.

We go wrong the moment we start correcting others, and we forget how we're dealing with ourselves. By the time we realise it, it is too late for anyone to understand why we were correcting them, and we lose them and start blaming ourselves. So to avoid this situation, we have to avoid the beginning of this cycle.

Yes, one thing for sure you can do is, even if you feel and your gut says that something is wrong, don't try to protect or correct anyone; just try to advise them, and if they take it, well and good, and if they don't, just open your arms wide for the time they're looking for someone to just hold them and hug them tightly. Don't blame them or yourself.

Everyone has their own journey; they will have ups and downs too, and you cannot walk someone else's journey; it is theirs, and you are a merry side character in their film.

Destiny and Decision

For me personally, destiny is above decisions, because anything that is meant for us comes to us in any way.

I always wanted to be a doctor and an actor if I got a chance to, but see, destiny had something for me. I couldn't continue my dream of pursuing medicine; instead, being an actor was destined to happen. It was like a platter served in front of me.

My decision was something that was influenced by the matchmaking of my destiny.

"Destiny" is like a magic spell that influences you, and when you start influencing this influence, it works for you. The moment you get influenced by it, the downward fall begins.

For anyone, it is very easy to say, "Oh, destiny has done wonders for you, or you have a good destiny." But trust me, that is not the case. If it is serving dishes to you on a platter, the other time it asks you to make a platter out of it, and imagine if you don't know how to cook! It is a new challenge all around.

What I have realised is that you should appreciate and respect what you get served and practice being served.

Your decisions are influenced by your destiny; even if you do not agree with this, that one time is still waiting for you ahead, or maybe it might have happened and you just didn't realise it. Just recall, realise, and appreciate it.

True and False

"Works for strong-minded folks who wish to live a pretty simpler life."

As kids, we have always answered the one-mark questions, where we answer "true or false", Those were the best days, if you ask me.

As we grow, we grow our complications as well. I know things are not going to be as simple as our childhood, but yes, they can be a bit simpler than what we've made right now.

Just recall yourself and think about how you used to answer every question so innocently with zero complications. It was because you were more focused and had fewer distractions, hence things seemed simpler.

Now just try to answer or try to handle any situation according to how it affects you; think about yourself.

The questions will be easier to answer, and the complications will be less than ever. It only works for strong-minded folks who wish to live a pretty simple life. The way of handling is the art of learning the true and false of life.

Consistency

"Is what brought them to their peak of success and happiness."

Being a part of today's generation, it is one of the hardest things to carry.

I look around and see hundreds of distractions. I wonder how many things are there to pull us back.

You must be going through this problem of "not being consistent." Don't worry because you have the solution for it.

We often blame the situations and the people around us for not being favourable to us. Give yourself a moment and ask, "Why did you not do it?" Then think about how you could do it, and keep the courage to accept that the path you chose has put you in a situation where you can ask yourself the question.

You could have been more flexible with yourself and pushed yourself to limit yourself.

Look back and see how much time you spent scrolling and saving the posts on social media. You admire people who are consistent in whatever they do.

You admire their hard-earned success, but you never admire how they got everything you admire.

Their consistency towards their goal in a situation where every plan became unplanned and they had to continue with their jobs no matter what is what brought them to their peak of success and happiness.

So, stay consistent. A simple statement with no good English

Optimism

The trendiest word on an Instagram bio

Trust me, I have seen hundreds of Instagram users using this word.

What does optimism mean? To be hopeful, that's it?

I don't really feel it means that. What it actually refers to in my dictionary is to stay hopeful with a lot of hard work. You can't be hopeful by just hoping for the best; you need to work for it, and when you gain confidence that what you're doing is the right thing, you become optimistic and imbibe optimism.

It becomes your lifestyle. The problem is that we search for meanings on Google or, rarely, in a dictionary.

When we practically implement something in our lives, we get results according to the way we tackle it. Every situation has a different method of understanding, and in the same way, before we add any word to our bio, we need to understand it deeply and learn about it with an open mind.

Expect the Unexpected

"We will do the best of whatever we can."

I knew this statement after I read Oscar Wilde, and I experienced this statement when I started living in the wild.

During the shoot of my debut film, Sumeru, we expected things to go smoothly, but then situations changed, and we weren't even prepared to expect the unexpected.

I am not elaborating on what happened there, but how my team and I overcame it was indeed unexpected. We had faith in ourselves that, no matter what, we would do the best of whatever we could. This was the thought we had in our minds.

"The unexpected" situation brought us all together, and we did the expected teamwork.

When you have faith in yourself and the people around you, you will overcome the unexpected.

What Others See

When you fail to see the best in you, see through the eyes of people who love you.

When you feel the lowest, remember how they admire you. When you fall down, remind yourself that they will always love to see you fighting. When all these energies of keeping you supreme merge, it will create an aura for you, where you yourself will start believing and start living for your betterment.

What others see and believe about us affects us greatly. Sometimes in a negative way, but when we change our perspective and stay on the positive side, everything will fall into place.

Progress

As long as we have a goal, we will progress.

An aim in life helps us to be more focused on everything we do.

A person who has a goal will take every step and every decision to reach closer to his or her goal.

A person with no goal will always jump from one place to another; he or she will have multiple thoughts and multiple goals, but neither of them is a goal to be accomplished. They are just thoughts.

The word progress has been mistaken; we assume it to be a better way of doing something that we weren't able to do once; instead, it is what we have learned from the not-so-perfect to one step towards perfection. It is something we have learned in the journey of reaching where we are willing to reach. The lessons you learn in between are your progress.

If you haven't learned anything, then you are still where you started.

There has been no progress, so to progress, keep your eyes and brain wide open along with your ears to become the best version of yourself.

Outgrow Yourself

Growing up means learning and listening to everyone's opinion. Being an older child, I had always been under the shadow of people around me. I had to listen to what every elder of the family thought and many other things that somewhat made me a lolled person because I thought my thoughts didn't matter much, thus keeping them to myself.

When I grew up, I realised how dependent and complex it had become for me to put my brain into words, and this troubled me a lot. I met new people, and I felt aloof inside.

You know that when you feel things are not for you, it is actually the thought that pushes you to make things turn in your favour.

My actions felt like I was keeping my word to become dominant, but that wasn't the case ever, and later on I rectified that my mannerism of expressing myself was quite dominant, which eventually affected my relationships in life.

I decided to find a way, and what I found was that the complex of feeling unheard made me loud and unclear about expressing my thoughts. I figured out that being the same won't help me, so I decided to change my ways and emphasise being less vocal and more into action. Eventually, growing my actions gave me the space to outgrow and explore myself, and trust me, even this action would not keep everyone happy, but yes, it does keep me on the edge of satisfaction, so why not?

We can give ourselves space and time to grow, rather than pressuring ourselves to do things at the speed of light.

We Compare

Can you imagine your dog comparing his way of life with yours?

No, not at all. God has created every creature with its own specialties, but what we have done to ourselves is something all of us need to realise.

An animal fights for a particular area or space for survival, but we humans try to possess an area so that we can compare it later with the other person. The "power of comparison" has led to half of the issues in our lives.

We are in a state of mind where we compare everything with the people around us, be it relationships, careers, money, or anything else. The superpower of humans has been limited to the materialistic things around us, because of this the self-success rate of an individual has dropped and the success rate due to comparison has increased.

We compare and grow these days; instead, we should grow individually to break the barriers of comparison. Each one of us should excel in our own way.

In the world of animals, there is no comparison; maybe that is the only reason that our pets seem to be better than us sometimes. We have lost our stability while running after the success of others; we are so tired of running the race that we forget our own capabilities and specialties. We were and are unique in our own way; all we have to do is stop comparing us with what influences us.

Ask Yourself about Yourself

As we get busy with work and time, we give up on certain things and start living with the circumstances around us. Basically, we surrender, and later we blame everything and say, "The time wasn't good enough!"

Like really? Is it so? The answer is an absolute no. You surrendered, my dear.

You fought for the situation and others, but never for yourself. Just ask yourself once and answer honestly because this is a question about you.

We are really careful about the work when we have to answer the boss, but never for ourselves. When we aren't answerable to anyone, we neglect things, and that costs us really well.

The moment you start doing things for yourself, you will see improvements around you. Just blaming and shouting at others will never help you; just accept that you have surrendered and neglected what was meant for you. No one is better judged for themselves than you.

So just keep yourself up, make commitments to yourself, and do it for yourself.

Mirror Work

When someone else tries to show us the mirror, we barely accept that. There are ego and anger issues once you try to show someone who they are and what they are trying to be, and it is absolutely normal.

Now I ask you: have you ever seen yourself in the mirror? As we grow up, we try to change others; we try to correct the mistakes of others. Even if it is goodwill, a person with complexes will get offended, and honestly, everyone has their own complexes, even you.

Instead of showing others the mirror, just try to sit back and express yourself in front of the mirror. I bet half of you won't be able to appreciate the way you are. Whatever you post on social media, it is a visual world, but when you see yourself practically, criticism and self-correction lie somewhere in the corner. What comes first is expressing yourself to yourself.

You need to give yourself the time and space to see what you were and what you have become and how things have changed within you.

Mirroring yourself would be a sign of growth, and when you grow, you inspire others to grow as well.

Preaching or Learning?

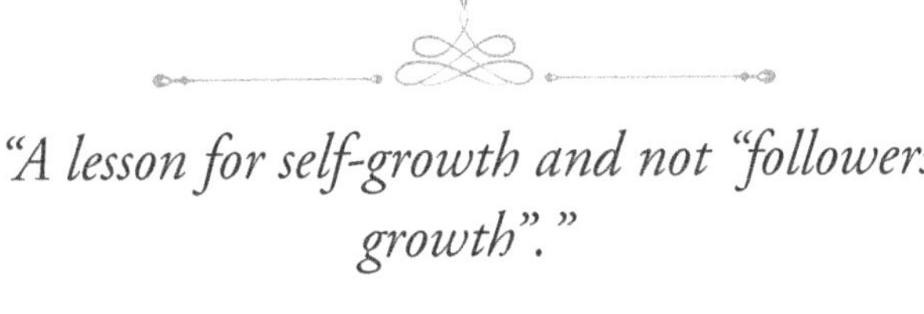

We live in a world where we share quotes but never implement them. You know, if we start learning from the little things in life, we won't require hours of scrolling on social media for the appropriate feeling that we want to express.

We share a quote for the followers who follow us; we want to preach to people; we want to tell them how wrong they are or how right they are, but we neglect our time and energy that could have been used for ourselves and our own learning.

I feel all of us need to work on ourselves to create a more humane environment for us to live longer. Every day is a new lesson to be learned—a lesson for self-growth and not "follower growth".

The moment we decide to learn and not preach, this world will be a more authentic place, a "realistic" one.

Preaching is worth it only when you follow it wholeheartedly; otherwise, it's just a business or a way of making yourself "great" in front of a handful of people.

You are The Treasure

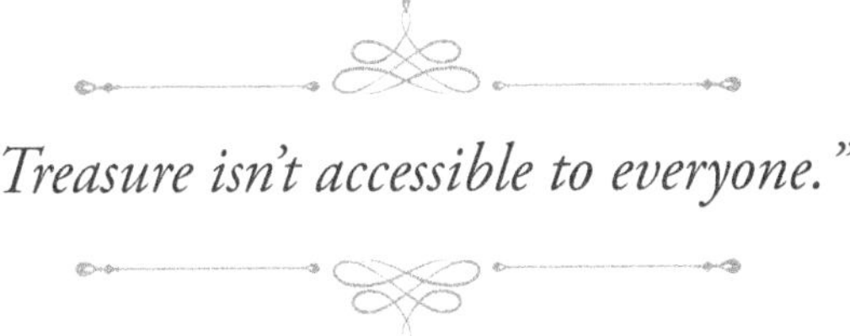

What is a treasure?

Something worth the wait, something everyone wants to have in their life, something everyone is looking for in their lives.

Since childhood, we have heard of treasure as something very special and fascinating, just like you.

Treasure is something that isn't easily accessible to everyone; people work hard to achieve it.

For you, your treasure lies within you. Work hard on yourself and dig out the treasure inside you. Once you find yourself to be your own treasure, anything and anyone who does not belong to you will be distant from you, because, as I said, treasure isn't accessible to everyone.

Anything or anyone who is seeking you will have to work hard to achieve you because you are the treasure; you can't be someone's random thing.

102

Accepting What Lies Within

"It is actually very close to realisation and learning."

It is difficult to accept our own faults; we blame others and then try to defend ourselves through the act of being "normal" when we realise our mistake.

At first, we need to accept that we are humans and that we make mistakes.

"Acceptance" is not only about accepting how people around us are; it is something much more than that. We have to learn how to accept our flaws and work on them. None of us can be flawless, but we can move a step forward by accepting the flaws that lie within us.

"Accepting flaws" does not mean I will stay the way I am; it is actually very close to realisation and learning, which brings you closer to "learning from the flaws" that are within you so that you don't repeat what wasn't appropriate.

Any change you expect from the world starts with you, and for that, you need to learn to accept your inner self and learn from your own flaws.

Lone Survivor

"If we can cross it halfway, we can make it full."

Whenever I look back, I see how far I have come, and even you need to realise that.

There are so many moments when we expect people to be around us. We want someone to tell us, "It will be fine, and it's all okay", but there's no one when we look around. It is a little hard for us to accept that; in fact, it breaks us more.

But you know what? As we try to find someone around in an ocean of expectations and miseries, we learn how to swim and survive in the search for "someone" we are looking for, but we neglect ourselves, and we never notice that we have been swimming and crossed halfway across the ocean.

We never realise how amazing lone survivors we've become. If we can cross it halfway, we can make it full.

And in case you find someone in the middle of the ocean, just be kind and helpful enough; you do not need to carry them on your back but to help them swim along to cross the other half.

This is what true lone survivors are: helpful, strong, and grounded. Keep going because there's a long way to go, and remember that nothing can stop you.

Togetherness

In a relationship, whenever we talk about "togetherness," it does not only mean we have to stay together or start things together; instead, it is the individual space we give each other to grow and explore ourselves so that we can reach a mark above everyone around us and stand together on top to cherish the moments that we have individually created.

Working on ourselves and reaching a point where we can proudly say, "We have created this moment together,"

In every relationship, this togetherness is necessary. If you apply your energy to your own growth, you will definitely reach where you want to, create your own space, help yourself, and reach the mark of togetherness in a relationship, all together.

Give the other person the space and time to create their own path, to reach the high point. Togetherness is a byproduct, because if you are already together, what next? How far will you practice togetherness? It seems special when you realise how far you have come working on yourselves, and now is the point where you can proudly say, "We built this individually for the sake of togetherness!"

To Inspire

When we talk of someone who has inspired us, we want to become like them; we admire them for who they are.

You know we don't get inspired by them; we are influenced by what we see about them and what they let the world see, but we never try to get the correct nerve. We wish we could also inspire others, but how?

You know that to inspire does not mean that you start teaching the world what is right and what is wrong. To inspire is to let the world see what difference you've made.

It is to learn from the changes other people have created and how hard they have worked to create this huge gap in their transformation journey. Learning from their handwork, dedication, and patience will make you admirable and "an inspiration" for millions of others.

You can be one of those people who inspire, but for that, you have to learn and make a difference in your lifestyle. To inspire, you have to be inspired by hard work and not by something someone has earned and achieved.

Knowing What You Need

*"You aren't a solution for everyone,
but for yourself."*

No one knows what you need, and no one cares whether you get what you need or not.

If you need to cry, do it; it makes your heart lighter and stronger; if you want to laugh, do it; it makes your throat clearer and heals your inner self; if you want to be angry, be it; your face and inner soul need to release that negativity that has a shelter in your heart.

Being with your own people makes you comfortable; being with strangers is an eye-opener, which should not make you underconfident but encourage you to be a better version of yourself.

Everyone around you is facing various issues and struggling for what they want. You might be keeping your worries to yourself, but the other person might not be, so be kind to however people react; it is their inner struggle that is making them the way they are. Everyone isn't like you, who can keep things to themselves.

You aren't a solution for everyone but for yourself. Know when you need to be with yourself; it makes you friendly with yourself. Know that you cannot be perfect; no one can be. Know that you can if you wish to do something.

Give Up or Give In

We know that it is much easier to give up on something than it is to make it happen.

To make things happen, it takes a lot of courage, faith, and willingness.

You give up when you lose all of them. It is said that whatever problem comes to us through the universe, the answer floats around us; it all depends on our willingness to have faith in our thoughts and keep moving forward with courage for the solution.

There will be a thousand reasons to give up, but then you have to find that one reason that makes you work harder, makes you more focused, and makes you more hungry to reach your goal.

What I Want

"The universe works on manifestations."

Not always will I get things that I want; not always will I get the solution to the problems that I'm facing; not always will I get a shoulder to cry on, but remember, "Not always will I be where I am right now."

I will make changes to the best of my abilities; I will create what I want; and till then, I will strive hard to make ends meet.

Maybe sometimes we feel alone, but then that is what we have been asking for—away from the chaos to be what we want to be. Recognise what you wanted; it is there; it's just that you aren't accepting the way it is coming to you because the universe works on manifestations and you get what you want. Nothing works against the law of manifestation.

The Last Note

Throughout the whole journey, I hope you remember every word you read and implement what suits you the best. We are all humans; we make mistakes and learn from them.

Maybe everything was too quick to happen in our lives, but then it happened for a reason and for us to learn and explore more about ourselves, our priorities, and how we balance everything.

We never kept our lives a secret; instead, we shared them with everyone around us. We made everyone a part of our lives, and in the end, we were thankless for every little thing life was giving us. Things change, and we are always looking forward to the change, therefore neglecting the present. Being thankful for every moment in the present and everything that happened is the true key to happiness, and to feel that happiness, we all should say the three magical words, "Thank You, Life", for everything.

See you all somewhere in the highs and lows of life. Take Care.

Love,

Sanskriti Bhatt.